20 WAYS TO DRAW A CAT

AND 23 OTHER AWESOME ANIMALS

JULIA KUO

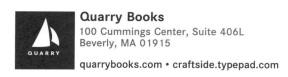

A Book for Artists, Designers, and Doodlers

Quarry Books
100 Cummings Center, Suite 406L
Beverly, MA 01915

quarrybooks.com • craftside.typepad.com

This library edition published in 2016 by Walter Foster Publishing,
a division of Quarto Publishing Group USA Inc.
6 Orchard Road, Suite 100
Lake Forest, CA 92630

Distributed in the United States and Canada by
Lerner Publisher Services
241 First Avenue North
Minneapolis, MN 55401 U.S.A.
www.lernerbooks.com

First Library Edition

Library of Congress Cataloging-in-Publication Data

Kuo, Julia.
   20 ways to draw a cat and 23 other awesome animals / Julia Kuo. -- First Library Edition.
      pages cm
   At head of title: Book for artists, designers, and doodlers
   ISBN 978-1-939581-71-6
   1. Animals in art. 2. Drawing--Technique. I. Title. II. Title: Twenty ways to draw a cat and 23 other awesome animals.
III. Title: Book for artists, designers, and doodlers.
   NC780.K86 2016
   743.6--dc23
                                                                        2015002419

012016
1780

9 8 7 6 5 4 3 2 1

CONTENTS

INTRODUCTION

Let's learn how to draw animals together! There are few things more fascinating and beautiful on Earth than animals. They come in all shapes and forms—from tiny birds to gigantic elephants, sweet deer to sly foxes, and striped zebras to spotted giraffes. You can pick your favorite animals from this book to draw, or you can think of animals that I haven't included. There are twenty-four different types of animals in this book, but that's just a tiny number out of all the animals out there! Next time you are at the zoo, keep an eye out for the unusual animals you haven't heard of before. For example, have you ever heard of a *capybara*? A capybara is the largest rodent in the world. That means it belongs to the same family as squirrels and bunnies, but it is as big as a dog!

Even the same types of animals come in so many varieties that it's impossible to draw them just one way. At first glance, a family of zebras might look very similar, but if you look closely you will notice that they don't have the same identical stripes. Think of yourself—you might look a little bit like the rest of your family, but you don't look exactly like them. Every single animal looks special in its own way, so I made sure that each drawing is a little different from the last.

HOW TO USE THIS BOOK

These drawings are all made up of a combination of lines, shapes, and patterns. Look for squares, circles, straight lines, and squiggly lines to help break down the pictures, and then try copying the different animal drawings using those simple elements. Draw the big shapes and lines first, and then add in the smaller details.

If you have tracing paper, you can trace the drawings directly, but don't worry about getting them exactly the same. When you think you have the hang of it, try drawing your own!

Try to start out with a pencil and eraser so that you're not afraid of making mistakes. When you feel more comfortable with drawing, explore by using many different types of tools—pens, colored pencils, markers, or even paints. It's always fun to try as many things as possible to decide what you like the best.

See how many different pictures you can come up with of your favorite animals. How many ways can you draw a turtle shell? You can make it a circle, square, or irregular shape. Think about what you can draw inside the shell. You can fill it with stripes, little spots, big spots, squares of different sizes, or just fill it in with a solid color. You can also decide to draw nothing inside the shell if you think it looks best that way, since sometimes less is more.

Don't forget to show your friends and family when you're done. Or even better yet, ask them if they want to make some drawings of their favorite animals, too!

sheep: marker and colored pencil
songbirds: marker and watercolor
rabbits: colored pencil
whales: watercolor

DRAW 20
cats

DRAW 20
TROPICAL BIRDS

DRAW 20
elephants

DRAW 20
Giraffes

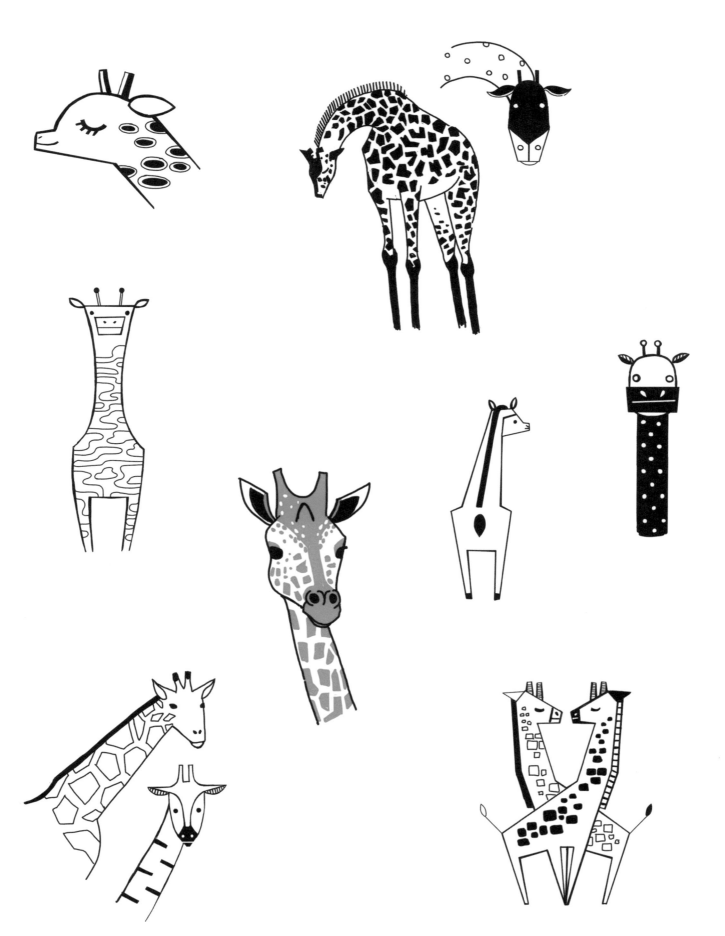

DRAW 20
BEARS

BUGS

octopi

DEER

DRAW 20
DOGS

DRAW 20
rabbits

DRAW 20
SQUIRRELS

TURTLES

Raccoons

DRAW 20
frogs

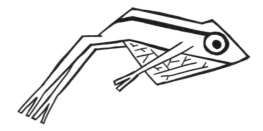

FOXES

hedgehogs

Kangaroos

DRAW 20
jellyfish

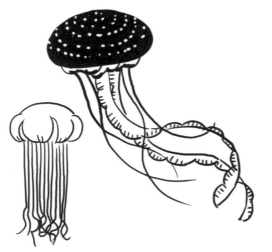

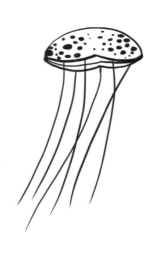
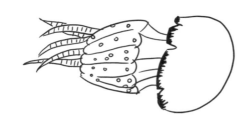
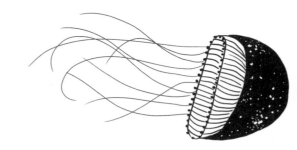
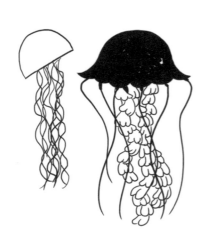

DRAW 20
ZEBRAS

DRAW 20
mice

DRAW 20
penguins & puffins

Skunks

PIGS

ABOUT THE ARTIST

Julia Kuo grew up in Los Angeles and studied illustration and marketing at Washington University in St. Louis. She currently works as a freelance illustrator in Chicago. Julia designs stationery, illustrates children's books, concert posters, and CD covers and paints in her free time. One of her gallery shows featured paintings of street fashion shots from Face Hunter. Julia's clients include American Greetings, the *New York Times*, Little, Brown and Company, Simon and Schuster, Capitol Records, and Universal Music Group. She is also part of The Nimbus Factory, a collective of two designers and two illustrators specializing in paper goods. Her illustrations have been honored in *American Illustration, CMYK* magazine, and *Creative Quarterly*. **juliakuo.com**